Transforming Our Schools

OUR WEALTH *is* WITHIN *each* STUDENT

Our Schools in Crisis?

Let's Get Practical

and Creative

LIFE LEARNING LLC

By Stan Ross

Transforming Our Schools - Our Wealth Is Within Each Student
by Stan Ross

© Stan Ross, Life Learning LLC
138 River Avenue, Mishawaka, IN 46544
Phone: (574) 255-2425 • E- Mail: LifeLearning@live.com

ISBN 978-0-692-00840-9
Library of Congress Control Number 2010903770

Back cover photo by Monte Draper

Printed in the United States of America

Table of Contents

Learnings Along the Way

The Source

If only my English teachers could see me now. I am drawn to the challenges of writing and away from my love of woodworking. The highlight of my school days and spare time at home was the joy of making things and exploring the great outdoors. Words were long a baffling problem for me. My parents read to Milt, my brother, and me nearly every evening as children, but I failed third grade due to my reading problems. Reading sessions with a private tutor were of little help. I disliked trading skiing, sledding and other natural boyhood activities for reading lessons.

Highlights of elementary school were kindergarten where we made carts from precut wheels, axles and boards, then pushed each other across the room. We also made "houses" and "forts" with block-like wooden boxes. During a fifth grade silent reading session, my teacher asked me if I would like to go to wood shop and work on my wall shelf project. I was gone. Another teacher, during a class reading assignment, asked me if I would like to work on our class viking ship project made of mattress boxes. I went to the front of the classroom where our four "oarsmen" creation was located and began work. What makes so few teachers do such unconventional fruitful things?

Failing third grade was one of the best things that happened to me. It gave me an extra year of maturity during the rest of my school career. It also put Milt, my brother, and me just one year apart in school. We really enjoyed sports and school together and later became shop teachers and coaches.

Because I lacked reading, writing and speaking skills, school was a struggle except for shop, math and sports. The most important reason for showing up in class to deliver a required speech was my ambition to earn a perfect attendance award. I received a lot of red marks on my written work.

As hard as I tried, grades above C's eluded me in classes requiring word skills until graduate school. I could hardly believe that I was not required to take remedial freshman English in college. As a freshman, my reading skills improved dramatically. It was either sink or swim in pursuit of a coaching and industrial arts teaching degree. I had to conquer nearly 500 pages of academic reading per week in order to survive the screening. I hadn't read 500 pages per semester in high school. I also had to do a lot of writing, which was always proofread and typed by talented fellow students. My lack of spelling and grammar skills would have done me in.

As a senior, I failed the upper division English test and had to remain after graduation to complete a "dumbbell" English class. The first four days, we had different teachers. The first three teachers told us they didn't want to teach the class and if we couldn't pass that simple test we shouldn't be teaching. We all knew our problems and only wanted help. Our fourth teacher stuck with us to completion and then turned us loose to become teachers.

Ironically, in the second year of my teaching, a publisher saw the work of my students and asked me to write a drafting textbook. The result became a widely used new approach to learning practical drafting skills.

During the last weeks of college, I made the rounds of various departments to get the required clearance signatures for graduation. At the speech therapy department, I was scheduled to receive therapy starting the next week. During the second session I was given this proposition, "If it is okay with you, due to the extent of your speech problem and the shortness of time, we will just sign you off for graduation." It was a deal and I was out of there.

So, in late summer I found myself hitch hiking from Indiana to California to begin my teaching and coaching career. According to the university, my speaking and writing skills were substandard. Luckily, teaching drafting and woodworking along with coaching track did not require much writing or lecturing. Fortunately, abbreviations are used extensively in drafting.

Due to teaching successes, I was asked by colleagues to share the techniques used in helping my students. The shop teachers did not care about the quality of my delivery. They just wanted to know what I did. My publishing editor said, "Stan, we don't care about your spelling or grammar just tell us what you do, we will make it right. You can write it on a paper sack if you like."

As my career progressed, I had gifted secretaries who cleaned up my writing. Finally, my written ideas were taken seriously. I learned a great deal about editing from Janet, my secretary, as she would move sentences and paragraphs to and from distant pages to improve the communication.

For me, running, mechanical aptitude, leadership qualities and practical creativity were like the trunk of my talent tree. As my talent grew, I naturally learned to write and speak. What I expressed was valued and I enjoyed sharing what I had learned. Before local, state and national groups, I consistently received high evaluations. Participants valued the subject matter and the simplicity of my delivery. Lack of eloquence kept me from making presentations complicated.

Difficulties in school gave me a great deal of empathy with students as they struggle. Learning problems led me in search for better ways to conduct schools. For some unknown reason, while in my classroom this thought came; "There has to be a better way to run a high school. What are you going to do about it? Earn an administrative credential and do something about it." As a result, I have had unusually fine opportunities to develop and share successful innovations.

I marvel at what people can do when their talents are tapped and cared for. The accomplishments of dedicated and creative people are wondrous. Yet, none of this would have been possible had it not been for nurturing each person's unique attributes. Sadly, the majority of us go through our entire life without experiencing the best of ourselves or life. Of all institutions, our schools are the best place for this process to take place.

I have deep concern and frustration regarding the conduct of our schools. Our schools lack care for the differing qualities of each student and community. This is very troubling as our prosperity depends upon the skills of each person to fulfill personal and community needs.

My offerings are based entirely upon my practical experience. I seek the simple essence of learning problems and solutions. Common words and simple language are used to convey the message in contrast to scholarly academic jargon. I try to write simply and significantly.

It is an absolute pleasure to share what I have learned with you. It is my hope that you will find what I offer especially useful. Our students and communities deserve a whole lot better than they are receiving from our schools.

Stan Ross
Author

Chapter 1
Orientation

Our greatest wealth is within the unique inborn abilities of each student. Nurturing these individual abilities is the most important thing our schools can do. Yet, this resource is virtually ignored in favor of government and university dictated academic standardized curriculum and testing. This regimented practice stifles personal worth; denying students and society of experiencing the wealth within each student. The loss is not measureable. It is beyond imagination. When their natural gifts are not engaged with useful activities, students miss the experience of passion in learning. What an awesome difference it would make if we were to develop the abilities within each student instead of trying to produce like performances through standardization. The particulars are intriguing and needs are achievable.

How can I love me if I don't know me?
How can others love me if I don't know myself?

Creativity is our greatest human asset. It is fueled by the quality and quantity of each person's learning. No other attribute approaches its importance to our well-being and prosperity. Creativity provides the means to solving the problems of life's ever changing conditions. We enjoy the abundant wealth within each student by nurturing their unique attributes in basic life experiences. The quality and quantity of learning is of great importance to our individual and collective future.

Quality learning entails an abundance of practical experiences considered "hands-on" or "down-to-earth" as contrasted with theoretical thoughts or abstract information. Accurate-to-life sensory, mental and muscular engagement results in quality learning. Activities that harmonize with each person's abilities produce the best results.

1

All highly creative achievements have been accomplished by people having a wealth of practical experience directly related to their accomplishments.

Practical experience is the natural way we develop from birth. As babies we learn by feeling, tasting, seeing, hearing, smelling and moving our muscles. Feeding, making sounds, sitting up, rolling over, crawling, standing up, walking and talking are all learned without instructions. These are considered monumental achievements yet they are only what can become a lifetime adventure.

Quantity of learning is produced by the diversity and depth of experiences. Variety provides greater opportunity to discover one's unique attributes. Diverse learning experiences are natural. From infancy we explore our surroundings as best we can. Babies eyes and head move about searching surroundings. Youngsters change activities impulsively when alternatives are available. Minutes with one activity and they are off sampling another.

Schools concentrate on students acquiring voluminous academic information at the neglect of applied skills. Without a practical experience base, information is less useful and theories are weak. Obsession with academics deprives our students of practical learning experiences greatly inhibiting creativity.

Years ago, while in my classroom, I was thinking about our schools' obsession with academics. Finally, my curiosity got the best of me and I sought the definition. My Webster Collegiate Dictionary revealed:

"Academic; theoretical and not expected to lead to useful results."

A surprise! Examination of the academic curriculum reveals that the education is not highly useful in daily life. Our lives require learning skills for daily needs followed by information which can enhance performance.

When I walk the halls of our high schools, I suppress my sadness and frustration over the waste of human potential. It matters not whether students are passing classes or sitting in classroom rows listening to their teacher or viewing textbooks and screens. Teachers are working hard, trying to accomplish their assigned tasks. Students simply go through the necessary motions to complete requirements. Every hour or so, in a mad scramble, the entire composition of the school population changes completely. Teachers lead different classes in a variety of subjects. Students change groups and participate in different subjects. Much of the learning lacks practical value for students. Nowhere does such a mix of people and activities take place because these practices are not very productive.

Schools are the most important institution we have for developing our most valuable resource, people. The students' learning is the most important factor to our personal and general welfare.

The reason students don't attend or do well in school is, they do not like the way they are treated.

Transformation of schools is absolutely necessary to realize the wealth within each student. By adhering to the natural ways of people and life we can optimize our limitless human potential. When each student's attributes are nurtured they become passionate learners. Their behavior becomes positive and the wealth within is realized.

Our schools can be made rewarding for all students and teachers.

Students are the greatest natural resource for accomplishing quality learning. Yet, they are scarcely involved in promoting learning with each other. Every good teacher knows there is a great deal of learning in the teaching process. Let's get the students involved in helping each other to maximize their learning.

Peer relationships are also a part of this strategy. Peers help each other more successfully than non-peers. They tend to be more honest and communicate better with each other. Support groups like Alcoholics Anonymous, Weight Watchers and others show the benefits of group relationships. Conventional school practices do not provide the conditions for students to help each other learn.

Transforming our schools involves much more than the way students and teachers relate. Curriculum too must change.

Focus is to be on basic life needs with regard given to addressing the diverse abilities and actual needs of students.

Now students are subject to standardized academic curricula, textbooks and tests dictated by governments and universities. The attempt is to produce high test scores. Content is based upon invalid assumptions coming from academicians and profit centered publishers of textbooks and tests. They are not based on real life needs. No regard is given to the diversity of students. The magnitude of this loss, due to these practices, is unimaginable.

There is agreement that our schools are not serving our students, communities or commercial needs adequately. The problems are not primarily the fault of our teachers, students or parents. Teachers are among the most dedicated, challenged and hard working members of our communities, yet they are undervalued. Teachers and students are assigned unrealistic tasks to accomplish under irrational conditions. The way our schools operate makes it extremely difficult to be successful in real terms, whether student or teacher.

To transform our schools, an understanding of the following is needed:

1) The core qualities of people
   a) Natural Diversity
   b) Personal Attributes
   c) Human Behavior
   d) Learning Capabilities
   e) Helping Each Other
   f) Group Activities
   g) Project Completion
2) What to learn
3) Conducting Programs

Natural Diversity

Everything in nature is diversified. No two things are ever alike. Each snowflake, grain of sand or ball bearing is different from all others. People are the most diversified of all things. We survive and thrive through diversity.

The benefits of diversity are threatened by the troubling movement toward segregation in our schools. Proliferation of charter, private, parochial and alternative schools exemplifies the attempts to isolate students from the advantages of natural diversity. Students are separated by academic "Honors," Advanced Placement and College Credit classes to the point that students of various backgrounds and abilities have little or no association with each other. Segregation breeds prejudice through ignorance of others. Sudents are being denied the opportunity to learn the richness of working together in diversity.

Personal Attributes

Each of us is born with an abundance of unique attributes. They are personal treasures to be discovered, developed, enjoyed and shared through life experiences. As students' talents are cultivated, learning becomes a passion.

Human Behavior

We have a primary psychological need for identity which is either positive or negative. Positive identity results in positive behavior while negative identity produces negative behavior. For positive identity we must readily receive and share, as well as, enjoy personal attributes. Negative identity results in either withdrawing from reality or expressing aggressive behavior.

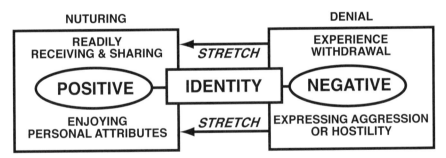

This Adlerian based psychological model of identity is the most useful and rewarding concept I have ever known. Use of its fundamentals virtually eliminates negative behavior and dramatically improves learning. Failure to use its fundamentals is the primary reason for our schools' shortcomings. This very important concept is detailed in Chapter 4; The Pattern of Human Behavior.

Learning Capabilities

Our human learning system is the finest of all our qualities. We naturally want to learn the things that are useful. Not wanting to learn is unnatural.
So, how do we learn?

This self-imposed question hit my brain like a hammer. I was dumbfounded for an answer. After years of university teacher training and experience, I could not define the process of learning. Gradually I created The Human Learning System concept.

The Human Learning System

Information is gathered by our senses and transmitted through sensory nerves to our brain where it is processed and stored. The brain releases information carried by motor nerves to our muscles. Muscle action expresses the information and focuses the senses on surrounding details. The senses, in turn, provide information for muscles to make accurate movements.

We can read and answer textbook mathematics problems using our eyes and simple hand movements to perfection in developing answers. Life mathematical problems are identified by using a variety of senses and solved by more complex muscular actions. Often they involve people, data, tools, instruments, machines and other products as with cashiering.

Accurate to real life activities of sensory and muscular involvement is essential for skill development and provides the essential "raw" material for creative accomplishments.

The wondrous human learning system is described in Chapter 5: How Do We Learn?

Helping Each Other

The ability to help each other is essential in the teamwork needs of daily life. Our prosperity and survival depends upon this skill. Helping each other in mixed groups of two to eight members develops understanding and concern for others. Learning is maximized, virtuous behavior is developed and prejudices are minimized resulting in productive and harmonious living. Helping each other through our experiences is neglected in our schools.

Group Activities

We learn and accomplish more in groups through sharing than alone. The strengths of each participant are used in teamwork to minimize individual weaknesses. A fundamental skill of group activities is communication.

Project Completion

Life is full of projects from small to very large. Some are done alone and others with partners or in groups. They can seem overwhelming. Through experience we learn the procedures for accomplishing ever more challenging undertakings. Successful completion of group projects depends on agreement of the purpose, procedures, resources and responsibilities.

What to Learn

The most important thing for each student to learn is the realization of their unique personal abilities in relationship to life needs. By focusing on Basic Life Activities the need for learning becomes apparent. These six Basic Life Activities are offered for consideration in curriculum development:

1) Good Self Health – Personal state of being
2) Employment Careers – Working at a job to earn money
3) Communication – Exchanging information
4) Social Relationships – Living and dealing with others
5) Environmental Harmony – Involvement with our surroundings
6) Aesthetic Enjoyments – Using or observing abilities in recreational and leisurely fashion

These are detailed in Chapter 6: What to Learn?

Conducting Programs

Using program management practices proven successful in everyday activities is needed in transforming our schools. Such practices are incorporated in The Management for Learning Concept composed of three program types:

1) Multi-purpose programs
2) Single purpose programs
3) Discussion programs

These are detailed in Chapter 7, Linking Students, Learning and Life

In starting my second teaching career my Superintendent agreed to let me teach Drafting I, II and III as well as Woodworking I, II and III each period everyday. Students were permitted to enroll any time throughout the year.

Using the Multi-Purpose Program component of the Management for Learning Concept, enrollment grew in two years to 185 students. The five classes averaged 37 students. The largest class of 45 proved to be one of my very best. Their accomplishments were great. The class practically taught it self. It was like a symphony as students in learning teams helped each other in harmony.

The problem of learning is not class size. More important is how the program is managed. We cannot afford to pay present salaries in order to achieve "optimum" class sizes of eight or ten students. By making use of the student resource of helping each other learn in larger classes we can afford higher salaries, improved facilities, better equipment and more supplies.

Learnings Along the Way

Regional Occupation Program

As the beginning Superintendent of the North Orange County Regional Occupational Program in Anaheim, California, I was able to part from tradition and utilize many innovative practices which proved to be very successful. During our forth year we served 10,000 high school and adult students in elective classes covering the full range of employment. Most of our classes were held in places of business with full time teachers from the respective trade at each site. Department stores, hospitals, auto dealerships, manufacturing plants, hotels, public safety facilities, super markets, nurseries and existing school facilities were used as Community Classrooms.

We had the finest of facilities with little capital expenditures in the best of learning environments. Students could enroll in any class at any time and withdraw as they chose without losing any credits. In this way they could find their niche. As a result, we had no administrative positions devoted to discipline or attendance problems, even though many of our students had behavior problems at their home schools. Our administration facility was leased from the Anaheim School District. Maintenance and remodeling was done by students with no outside contracting. The things we learned are useful to all school situations: many are shared here.

Chapter 2
Our Schools in Crisis?

Our schools are in monumental disarray over what the real problems are. Considering what our students achieve in comparison to their capabilities, our schools are in crisis. The difference between our students' accomplishments and their potential is truly beyond imagination. It is a crisis when students do not experience the wealth within their personal attributes. Our schools are not succeeding at an acceptable level. The extent of the problem is less apparent. It suffices to say the solutions are challenging and answers are urgently needed.

It is usually concluded that our students are falling short in comparison to students in other modern countries according to standardized academic test results. It is assumed that such tests have validity to real life needs, which they do not. A thorough examination of our school situation results in a considerably different conclusion.

Here you can expect an insightful examination of our schools with problems identified and practical solutions offered.

> *We will not enjoy the best of life until*
> *we enjoy the best of each individual.*

We are going down the wrong road with our students. The road we are taking attempts the impossible, the standardization of student performance. It is a straight and narrow highway without deviation. The need is for a network of roads that travel the wide open countryside accommodating the diversity of individual interests, abilities and needs.

As I visit the schools and long afterward, I agonize over the waste of student and teacher abilities. I know first hand the wonderful learning opportunities that can be made available to students and teachers. Activities in which personal attributes and useful skills are realized. I have witnessed thousands of students and hundreds of teachers respond with enthusiasm and positive results when the situation is conducive to effective learning.

It is tragic how we fail to experience the individual and collective best in individuals. This is due to our failure to nurture each other. It is only through our schools that this great neglect can be corrected. If not addressed in our schools, then where better is it to be done?

The problems of our schools are not the fault of our teachers, students or parents. Teachers are "qualified" by university training and state licensing. It results in licensing individuals who are not well suited for the profession. The way our schools are operated makes it extremely difficult to experience real success whether student or teacher.

Lack of good parenting is often to blame for the difficulties of our schools. This may be true but it is also true that just a few years ago today's parents were in school. In their schooling they did not have any learning experiences involving marriage relationships or the nurturing of children.

Students are certainly not the real problem for they are products of their families and communities. In fact, the problems of our schools are not the fault of any person or group. The problems of our schools have accumulated over years with many factors contributing to the mounting failures.

I have visited with innumerable people from many walks of life regarding the state of our schools. Never have I found disagreement with the need for substantial changes in our schools. Educators and legislators have not made the necessary changes. Well intentioned efforts have generally worsened the situation.

Secondary schools: public, parochial and private have become prep schools for government and university imposed standardized test taking instead of prep schools for life.

Schools operate like manufacturing factories as they try to produce students who are to achieve high test scores. In the process students and teachers are expected to perform like robots, instead of serving each student's learning needs. The innate wealth of both students and teachers remains unrealized.

Indicators of the School Crisis

The most apparent problem is our 30% or more national average high school dropout rate. In large cities and among some minority populations the dropout rates exceed 50%. There is absolutely no worthy excuse for such high rates. Our dropout rates are a travesty. Standardized test results and dropout percentages do not reveal the real problems.

Students are denied the opportunity to explore basic life activities. As a result they can not discover, develop, enjoy and share their personal treasures. It is unlikely they will ever experience the best of themselves and gain a genuine sense of self-worth as a result of their school experiences.

How can students experience a sense of self-worth when
their attributes remain neglected?

When we fail to nurture the attributes of each student, we cannot expect the individual to value themselves or others. The results are:

1) Deplorable dropout rates
2) Escalating health problems
3) Lack fo employment skills
4) Degeneration of family relationships
5) Substance and physical abuse
6) Absurd incarceration rates
7) Financial indebtedness
8) Environmental degradation
9) Material greed

Many students are not able to perform needed skills upon leaving school. These problems include:

1) Personal Health – Students do not learn the practices of good exercise or consumption in school. Health problems and costs are increasing at alarming rates. The most effective way to reverse our health care problems is practicing proper exercise and nutrition. Good health habits should be a primary lesson in schools.
2) Employment Skills – There are few if any school experiences that help students make valid employment career choices. Most students leaving

school have no idea what employment career opportunities or goals they want to pursue. They do not have the opportunity to develop the basic skills needed for the diversity of employment opportunities.

3) Family Values – Schools offer little or no experience for making good marriage relationships and nurturing children. Students have twelve years of social studies and not one week is devoted to marriage relationships or nurturing children. What could be more important?

4) Financial Management – Learning experiences involving handling budget, debt, savings and investments are lacking. In fact, universities now we have multiple generations of irresponsible indebtedness.

5) Teamwork Skills – Short, are group experiences involving problem identification, planning and carrying out solutions related to life.

6) Academic Learning – Students lack ability to apply academic subjects in life situations. Students are long on information and short on useful skills.

7) Compulsive Consumption – Debt and landfills grow while saving rates decrease. Material status, symbols and labels are sought in lieu of genuine value.

8) Environmental Care – Understandings and actions to live in harmony with our environment are deficient.

Causes of Our School's Problems

Government Mandates

Our Federal and State governments have mandated standardized academic curriculums, textbooks and testing. This practice suppresses maturation of personal attributes and ignores practical experiences that are essential for creative accomplishments. These practices have turned the focus of our schools on standardized dictates instead of serving the individual needs of students and their wealth within.

No Child Left Behind is the worst thing that ever happened to our schools. It has nationalized our public schools to the detriment of students, teachers and their communities. This is happening in a nation that advocates individual freedom. According to our nation's constitution everyone has the right to pursue their own happiness. No Child Left Behind denies students the freedom and rightful opportunity to experience the best of themselves.

This act is the capstone of a repressive process started years ago. Government has increasingly imposed standardization of learning on schools. The process has grown over the years and its effects are dangerous to our welfare.

No Child Left Behind was promoted with fraudulent claims of success in Texas. It was enacted by many well meaning legislators who were trying to be helpful. As a result, textbook and test publishers have a "cash cow." We are training a generation of standardized test takers with undesirable results. Teachers and students have become like robots serving the dictates of the governments rather than attend student and community needs. Individuals and communities have no say as to what is best for them. It matters not whether rural or city, slum or suburban, seaside or mountain side; "You are all the same." Governments should facilitate local school initiatives for improvements instead of dictating standardization. This can be done by funding promising projects initiated by local communities and providing information about successes.

No Child Left Behind has resulted in ***all children left behind***. It has proven to be good for driving students out of school and fostered the "I'll just get by" attitude.

Unfortunately, Federal and State governments seem determined to continue down the same wasteful and destructive road, even though their mandates are not working.

As long as we violate "natural laws" our students will fail to experience real success. The fundamental question is, "Are we to thrive through the laws of ***government*** or the "laws" of **nature**? There is a conflict. The contrasts are as follows:

1. *Standardized* vs **Diversified**   4. *Commonality* vs **Creativity**
2. *Academic* vs **Practical**   5. *Competition* vs **Cooperation**
3. *Regimentation* vs **Freedom**   6. *Segregation* vs **Integration**

When we deny the "laws" of nature we cannot experience genuine success.

University Requirements

Like government mandates, university required high school curriculum and standardized testing stifles individuality and the practical learning experiences needed for creative accomplishments. Colleges are now creeping into our students' high school experience with college credit courses. These practices produce the detrimental effects of segregation in which both personal superiority and inferiority generate. The opportunities for the "best and brightest" and the "rest" to know each other are inhibited, which is lessening for all. The practices also crowd out comprehensive learning experiences, including; fine arts, good self health practices, employment career skills, social relationships, communication skills and environmental care.

University curriculum and testing requirements leave much to be desired in determining success, as college drop out rates rival the troubling rates of our high schools. A disturbing percentage of students leaving college have difficulty with employment and a great deal of debt.

Fortunately there is a growing trend away from use of test results in determining college entrance.

> TIME magazine, June 9, 2008 reports that 456 accredited colleges and universities no longer require the SAT or ACT tests for any applicants. These schools have dropped standardized test requirements because they feel:
>
> 1) That the SAT and ACT aren't an accurate measure of a students ability.
> 2) That high school classroom performance is a better indicator of success.
> 3) That standardized tests deter some minority and low-income students from applying.[1]

It seems our government and universities are determined to continue down the same unproductive and destructive road.

Parents, students, citizens and educators know a lot more about their student and community needs than distant governments and universities. Governments and universities should facilitate local school improvements instead of dictating standardization. Financial equity is needed for communities and students. The government should protect freedom for our schools, just as it should protect freedom in our churches and homes.

[1] "The World," *Time*, June 9, 2008

Standardization

It is absurd to think that personal performance can be accurately measured with standardized written short answer tests.

Schools are virtually the only place in society where such standardized testing is done. In other settings, evaluation is done primarily through personal observation of actual performance by experienced individuals. Standardization serves to regiment students and teachers alike. Attempts to standardize performance, is a fundamental totalitarian practice, although likely not intended to do so in the case of our schools. Leaders and legislators advocate freedom on one hand and too often, suppress it on the other. These are disturbing trends. In our rapidly changing world, the fostering of individual ingenuity has a far better economic prospect.

Government and university requirements have led to growing segregation within and among our schools. The proliferation of charter, private, parochial and alterative schools increases segregation. Honors, Advanced Placement and Advanced College Placement classes classify students in a competitive process that restricts understanding of others. The more alike we are "made" to be the less we have to offer each other. Segregation lessens our understanding and ability to share. It impedes empathy for others, preventing us from knowing our fellow brothers and sisters.

This is not to say that standards are not important. Standards are important when properly used. To be most useful they must fit the resources and needs of specific situations such as health and safety considerations.

Academics

The New Oxford American Dictionary definition:

> *"Academic; not of practical relevance;*
> *of only theoretical interest."*

Our lives require useful skills followed by information which can enhance our performances. The practical experience gained through life activities is vital to successful creative accomplishments. All highly creative people have had a wealth of practical experience in their field of accomplishment.

It is mystifying why academics are so aggrandized. All of the government and university mandates have centered on the academic subjects; English, mathematics, science, social studies and foreign languages. Academics are revered in schools. They dominate the school environment. The academic stress is perpetuated by universities in teacher training, government mandates and the traditional curriculum. Students are classified and ranked according to their performances in the academic subjects. In reality teachers are ranked according to the subjects they teach.

It is also a wonder why so much status is given to "hard" or "solid" subjects. When a subject is made difficult, it is given high status in schools. It seems logical that acquiring skills should be made as easy to learn as possible so the students can enjoy their use. It is saddening to observe how little of our students' innate capabilities will ever be experienced because of academic dominance. These practices establish a competitive atmosphere which is detrimental to sharing.

Textbooks

Nearly every class has textbooks. It's the thing to do in schools. Is this the best practice for promoting quality learning? Is it the most desirable use of financial resources? Might the money be better spent purchasing a variety of literature, equipment and supplies related to learning activities?

Standardized textbooks do not serve the diverse needs of students. At best, they deliver a particular slant with their content. Too often textbooks indoctrinate bias view points. This unwholesome attempt is best countered by experiencing a variety of view points, enabling students to develop their own understandings and beliefs from their communications.

On March 12, 2010, the Texas board of education voted 10-5 in favor of curriculum standards that would promote conservative issues in pages of the state's textbooks. The changes included an increased emphasis on and sympathetic treatment of such Republican touchstones as the National Rifle Association and the Moral Majority. They also tout the superiority of capitalism and the role of Christianity in the nation's founding. Some board members were less than fond of Thomas Jefferson's ideas of separation of church and state.

Since the 1970s, the state has dropped books that were seen as too liberal or anti-Christian, to omit passages on the gay-rights movement and tone down global-warming arguments.

As one of America's largest textbook buyers, the Longhorn State has a good deal of sway over what's peddled to schools nationwide.[2]

School Operation

Schools are operated like no other enterprise. No place else in our society are participants and activities conducted in such an unproductive manner. In a mad scramble, every hour or so, the whole school population changes locations, activities and personnel. Supervisors in other organizations are not directly responsible for groups of 20 or more people changing five or more times per day. They are not responsible for conducting as many as five different activities with five different groups of 20 or more members per day. Leaders are not required to evaluate the work of 120 participants on a daily, weekly or monthly basis. Some teachers lecture, nearly an hour, three to five times a day, five days per week. Church ministers preach a 25 minute sermon one to three times per week. Would youth leaders and Little League coaches like to handle five different teams per day five days per week in different activities or sports?

Schools are operated in a manner that is degrading to participants. The practices are not used by other enterprises because they are not effective. The operation is unnatural to the inherent qualities of people. People instinctively work together in manageable size groups where rapport, trust and appreciation are established in teamwork. This is not possible in the traditional school operation. Students are not learning the benefits and responsibilities of teamwork.

Leadership

There is a lack of practical, visionary and courageous leadership in our schools. Administrators are so busy trying to make the system work, conform to new fads and uphold the program that little is left for envisioning and

[2] Kayla Webley, "The Textbook Wars," *Time*, March 29, 2010, p 14

implementing needed changes. Due to habitual practices, educators are seemingly unable to understand the magnitude of school problems and seek answers. In fact, there is substantial resistance to change.

Educator Education

Universities and colleges train all teachers, counselors and administrators as well as legislators. These institutions do not accept the responsibility for the shortcomings of our schools, nor do they respond to the needs in productive ways. Universities are considered research centers where problems should be identified and solutions developed. They fail in regard to our schools. Their solution to our schools' problems is to require more university training for educators. This is not improving our schools. However, it does increase university enrollment and income.

> *When will the universities be held responsible for*
> *the performance of their certified educator graduates?*

We could do well to revise our complete educator preparation, selection, certification and salary program. Our present system leaves much to be desired. It is questionable whether universities are capable of preparing educators to serve student and community needs.

Summary

In practice, our schools primarily serve the ill-found dictates of the government and requirements of universities. In reality, they should serve the needs of students and society.

Common understanding for the operational purpose of schools has historically been elusive. Clearly defining why programs exist is a very challenging and rewarding endeavor. It brings clarity to complexity and focuses resources economically. This very important process is offered in the next chapter, "Why Have Schools?"

Learnings Along the Way

U.S.O.E. Visits N.O.C.R.O.P.

The United States Office of Education learned of our North Orange County Regional Occupational Program success in California and a group of their officials toured our classes. Impressed with the innovation they designated our program as a model for the nation. Before leaving our offices they asked, "How much money do you need?" I replied, "We don't need any money as we are actually developing a surplus." Disappointingly, we never heard from them again as we wouldn't help them disperse their grant money.

Midnight Math Class

Ted worked the day shift at the 35,000 employee Rockwell International-Space Division, maker of the Apollo Spacecraft in Downey, California. He voluntarily taught a midnight basic mathematics class Tuesdays and Thursdays to employees coming off the second shift. I arranged for him to be paid for his work and for the students to receive high school credit for their achievements. We were both excited about the arrangement. The next class meeting Ted took the necessary school forms which his students completed. We are all set . . . No!

At the next class meeting only one-third of the 18 or 20 students showed up. Normally only two or three students at most would be absent. What went wrong? Ted made the rounds during second shift to find the answer. There were two primary reasons the students did not come to class:

1. For some students previous school experiences were so negative that they choose never to have any school connected activities again.
2. Other long time employees were afraid the company would fire them if it were learned that they hadn't graduated from high school.

I asked Ted how these successful employees got their job in the first place. He found that they put the name of a high school that no longer existed or they used a school in a distant state. What would you do, if with a family, you needed a job and were repeatedly passed over for less able applicants?

Awards Program

The idea of giving awards to shop students at the end of school year during the school's Awards Program was accepted by the administration. It only took three afternoons to obtain $2,500 in donations from local businesses and individuals for purchasing tool awards. The largest donation was $250 and the smallest $25. Only one person failed to donate. There is great grass roots support for hands-on experience. The students cherished their tool awards. It was really a joy to see these students recognized before the entire student body. The next year however, the administrator in charge said we should have a separate shop awards program. We thought our shop students should be considered within the entire student body. Sadly, that ended the shop awards program.

Chapter 3
Why Have Schools?

This question was one of the most provocative and rewarding questions ever asked of me. In a discussion with Jack Rush, head of management training at Rockwell International - Space Division in Downey, California, I was asked, "In a single sentence, why do we have schools?" My immediate thoughts seemed trite. A reasonable answer eluded me for weeks. Like a high school geometry problem, I could not let go of the question. Gradually, an answer began to form.

The single, simple sentence condition of why an activity should exist is called an Operational Purpose Statement. Such statements are challenging to develop but well worth the effort. They focus enterprises and resources upon a precise goal.

Currently, Mission Statements are fashionable. They are generally rather long and rambling statements that serve as little more than window dressing.

One of the finest single simple sentences was President John F. Kennedy's; "We will send a man to the moon and return safely within the decade." Due to its definitive simplicity, the statement resulted in one of the greatest scientific development periods in history was launched.

Over many years, my original thoughts concerning why we should have schools have changed.

Now I think:

*"Our schools are for students to help each other **learn** to enjoy their personal attributes in basic **life** activities."*

Originally, consideration was given to educate and teach. I had witnessed a lot of teaching and education being done without great results. Why are we educating or teaching? Learning is the purpose.

The words *learning* and *life* have always been in each refinement. The most recent inclusion is *help each other*, which is the best way to promote learning. It is the fundamental skill for teamwork and the means to developing virtuous behavior habits.

Helping Each Other Learn

Human beings naturally congregate or gather in groups. This is done so we can help each other by sharing. The strengths of each participant are utilized and cover individual weaknesses. In doing so, more can be accomplished for the good of all. Helping each other is most fundament to the success of group activities. It is the best way for an individual to attain the sense of self-worth and change negative behavior into positive behavior.

In our Regional Occupational Program hundreds of high school students were involved in helping underachieving elementary pupils to develop reading skills. Many of the older students were poor achievers with behavior problems at their school. In a sizable study, elementary and high school students were tested before and after the program. They were also tested months later to determine their retention. Test results indicated the most improvement of any previously used reading improvement program. This was true for both the elementary and high school students. Within a short time in the program the behavior of both older and younger participants changed from negative to positive. The behavior changes were the most dramatic I have ever seen, as students gained a greater sense of self-worth.

Youngsters do not generally differentiate between "good" people and "bums." "Little" people enjoy the attention of "big" people. "Little" people do not judge the appearance of "big" people. "Bums" thirst for attention. They crave the self-worth expressed to them by "little" people. With mutual admiration, bonding is established. The high school student may occasionally skip high school but will not miss helping their "little" friend. The lagging elementary pupil will not miss school because a "big" friend is there to help with learning.

This activity is especially effective because both participants struggle with reading. In this way, they are peers. Typically schools deal with this by allowing only the "good" high school students to help. This practice is not as effective because "good" students have not encountered great difficulty in learning. By partnering students with similar problems, peer relationships are established. Peer groups have proven to be an effective way of learning improved behavior. Alcoholics Anonymous, Weight Watchers, Gamblers Anonymous and other support groups are proven examples. Schools do not use this practice to any significant degree and clearly have the need.

Every good teacher knows their own learning is maximized from their experiences with students. Students help the teacher learn due to their difficulties. This is why it is important to have students help each other learn. Trying to play strictly the teacher role, or the learner role, is inefficient and unnatural. Helping another learn is a most effective way to develop a personal sense of self-worth as well as communication and social skills.

Personal Attributes

It is important for students to enjoy their own and others' unique personal attributes. Personal attributes are the soul of us. They are what we are; our identity and treasure. Neglecting them is dehumanizing and leads to negative behavior. Unfortunately, our schools focus on standardization of learning at the neglect of nurturing student attributes.

There are four important things to be considered when developing a learning program:

1) Human Behavior
2) How We Learn
3) Basic Life Activities
4) Fundamental of Program Development

Each consideration is detailed in the next chapters.

Summary

Acceptance of these premises necessitates an entire transformation of our schools. The changes do not need to be expensive but will require agreement on the need for change as well as commitment to the purpose and the process.

Chapter 5
How Do We Learn?

Learning is the life blood of human activity.

The most important thing we can do is learn. It is nature's finest gift and our greatest asset. Humans learn better than any other creature or any device. It is perfectly natural for us to want to learn. Understanding how we learn is important to everyone, especially in conducting schools.

As a university-trained and dedicated teacher, it is puzzling to me how little I understood in my early career about human learning. When I made the decision to include learning in my operational purpose statement for schools, I didn't realize the profound effect it would have on future experiences. Including learning, challenged me to answer this simple self-imposed question, "How do we learn?" I had no good answer so I started searching my experiences for an answer. The results of my never-ending quest have been very rewarding for students, associates and me.

We each have a Human Learning System that operates in the same basic manner with varying qualities from person to person. No two persons' ability to learn is alike. Some students learn some things early. Others may learn the same things later with great success, thus, "late bloomers." The amazing Human Learning System is composed of five subsystems: 1) Senses, 2) Sensory Nerves, 3) Brain, 4) Motor Nerves and 5) Muscles.

The Human Learning System

Our **Senses** gather millions and millions of bits of information from the environment to which they are exposed. The **Sensory Nerves** transmit information from the senses to the brain. Our **Brain** evaluates, decides, stores, processes, creates and releases information to the motor nerves. The **Motor Nerves** carry information released from the brain to the muscles. Our **Muscles** respond to produce information transmitted from the brain. Each of these subsystems varies markedly from individual to individual, yet the total system operates in the same general manner for all of us.

Our Senses

Our senses gather all the information used in learning. They also monitor our muscular movements in making precise movements. We have these six senses:

1) **Touch** is accomplished through our skin to detect temperature, sizes, pressures, textures and shapes.

2) **Sight** is the most useful sense for learning. We distinguish light, distances, shapes, movements, shades, patterns, colors and textures.

3) **Hearing** provides reception of voice, music's beauty, nature's sounds and activity noises.

4) **Smelling** enables enjoyment for the scents of flowers, perfume, food and nature. It can detect fires, gases and spoilages.

5) **Taste** provides the pleasures of food and may detect helpful or harmful elements.

6) **Balance** enables us to freely move about and gain exposure to the variety and quantity of our surroundings. Balancing is the neglected sense as it is usually considered as part of the ear due to the proximity. Its development is exceedingly important for success in learning.

Balancing may be considered as the orientation of our compass. The sense of being balanced and oriented allows learning experiences to flow through the learning system in an organized manner. Without balance, our compass wobbles in confusion. Information flows in a disorganized way, making learning experiences less effective. This is a serious and growing problem among our youth. Watching television, cell phone, computer and electronic game screens has worsened this situation.

Enhancing the sense of balance is called perceptional motor skill development. There are performance tests for detecting balance problems and prescriptive activities for improvement.

Balance is developed by walking beams, logs, fences and rails as well as riding non-motorized scooters, skating, gymnastics, bicycling, hop scotch, jumping rope, tumbling and wrestling.

Information gathered by the senses is transmitted by the sensory nerves to the brain.

Our Brain

Our brain evaluates, decides, stores, processes, creates and releases information. Data entering our brain is evaluated by our beliefs which greatly affect learning. The importance of beliefs is considered later in this chapter.

The greatest miracle of our brain is its creative ability. Random access to all information in the brain enables creativity. The quality and quantity of our learning experiences provide the substance for this distinctive ability. The accuracy of the sensory input and muscular responses, relative to real life experiences, determines the quality of learning. Practical, "hands-on," experiences of life provide the raw material for creativity.

Information is released from the brain to the motor nerves for transmission to the muscles.

Our Muscles

Muscles produce all information leaving the brain related to learning. The quality and quantity of information produced is dependent upon the skill, strength and endurance of our muscles. Without muscular movement information cannot be produced from the brain. For example, without moving any muscle try to give the answer to 2+2= __. All ways of producing or communicating the answer require muscular action. Muscles also move or focus our senses into positions so they can better gather information. Use of our muscles is extremely important to effective learning.

All music we hear and things we eat, wear, read, write and build require skilled muscular movements. Activities such as gymnastics, diving, swimming, dancing and other athletics involve nearly all of our muscles.

Our Hands

Hands are the most wondrous of our muscle systems. They feed us. Hands, along with our voice, produce words and numbers. As youngsters learn to print, they are able to produce graphic words and numbers. With cursive writing, they are able to increase the flow of words. Proper use of keyboards substantially increases word production and improves reading and writing abilities. Texting emanates from our hands. Use of stenotype coupled with a computer speeds the word flow dramatically. The increased productivity is due to the skill of our hands.

It is through the skill of our hands with pencils, pens, brushes, tools, machines, keyboards and musical instruments that useful information is produced. Production of art, crafts, cooking and cleaning as well as mechanical, medical, retail, construction, gardening, and farm work all involve the hands. It is with skilled hands that musicians produce beautiful music. Notice the hands of musicians as they play their instruments. Fantastic! In making precision machines the most precise straight and flat surfaces in metal are made by hand.

Next to our eyes and ears, our hands are the greatest gatherers of information. Hands also feed information to the brain through the sensitivity of the skin. One can even read and "talk" with the hands as with Braille and sign language. It is marvelous what skilled hands can do.

Hand use is a greatly neglected skill in our schools. There is a pervasive attitude that students who "aren't good with their brain" should learn to do something with their hands. "Academic" students are denied opportunities to develop fine hand and muscular skills. In fact, activities involving muscular movement are very often shunned by academia. It is unfortunate that many activities involving muscular movements are considered second rate. Reduction of playground time, physical education classes and general movement has added to learning and living problems.

THE HUMAN LEARNING SYSTEM

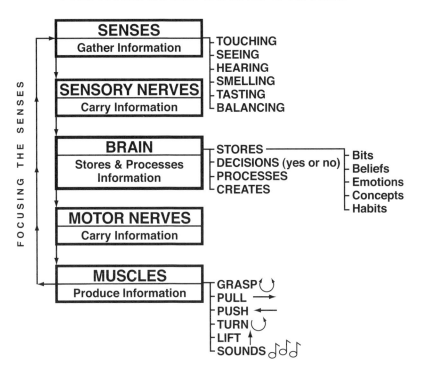

Quality of Learning

Unfortunately, our school focus is upon "feeding" student brains alone with information. Quality learning must involve the total learning system in accurate to life experiences. It is a contact "sport," contact with the real thing.

Involvement of the senses, brain and muscles must be accurate to life activities. We cannot expect quality learning when the sensory input and/or the muscular responses are not true to life needs. For example, we cannot learn to swim by listening to lectures, reading books, watching screens and passing written tests. We may gain a lot of information about swimming but are unable to perform in the water. These abstract experiences involved seeing and hearing while muscular activity was restricted to finger, hand and arm movements in testing. Swimming involves primarily the sense of touch and nearly all body muscle action in water. Abstract learning will not keep us afloat in water or life. Learning to swim does not enable us to read, although it may provide the desire to improve our swimming by reading.

How is it that our most intelligent, accomplished, students can complete two to four years of a foreign language receiving A's and not be able to carry on basic conversation? This is due to abstract learning based upon textbook knowledge instead of actual speaking skill development. The sensory involvement is with sight instead of hearing. Written words are processed in the brain rather than sounds. Muscles of the hands are used in place of the voice. The quality of practical experience is missing.

It is natural to acquire practical experience followed by shared information. As infants mature they learn through practical experiences naturally. Acquiring a great deal of information before practical experience is like getting the cart before the horse.

Of extreme importance is the fact that a wealth of practical experience is essential to productive creativity. Highly creative accomplishments have been achieved by individuals possessing an abundance of practical, "hands-on," experience.

The Shakers made a practice of each member learning two trades. They were an American communal religious group of more than 5,000 members active largely during the 1800s. The Shakers are considered the most inventive group per capita of all time. Certainly the wealth of practical experience gained in acquiring the skills of two trades greatly influenced their creative accomplishments.

Beliefs and Learning

Beliefs greatly affect one's learning. They are derived from lifetime experiences. Information fed into our brain is filtered by personal beliefs.

Like louvered blinds our beliefs accept, reject or modify the information as it enters our brain. If experiences have been wholesome, our beliefs will be receptive. Unwholesome beliefs will reject good learning opportunities. Usually information is modified to some degree. To acquire wholesome beliefs, personal attributes need to developed in virtuous experiences.

Virtues are considered good and desirable qualities in one's behavior. They are standards or guide-posts upon which we can develop wholesome beliefs.

Here are seven virtues for consideration in developing beliefs and conducting life activities:

1) **Initiative** – The power to begin. To try.

2) **Reverence** – The showing of deep regard. Care for self and surroundings.

3) **Honesty** – Being truthful. Performing with integrity.

4) **Curiosity** – The desire to learn. Wanting to find out.

5) **Compassion** – The understanding of others. Showing empathy, interest and concern for the cares of others.

6) **Gratitude** – Expressing sincere thankfulness. Demonstrating thanks with words and deeds.

7) **Generosity** – Freely sharing with others.

By practicing these virtues we can modify our beliefs to improve learning and lead a purposeful, fulfilled and happier life.

Summary

It is obvious that our schools are not providing students with the programs necessary for experiencing the quality of learning they need. What a tremendous difference it would make if personal learning needs were served, starting with practical life experiences.

Learnings Along the Way

Passion for Learning

Kayaks to the Colorado River

My students chose as a class project to make fiberglass kayaks for a float trip on the Colorado River. None of us had any fiber glassing experience. Tradesmen told us that due to the complexity of the proposed project we would not be successful in accomplishing our goal. Undaunted, we built the pattern for making the deck and hull molds. Students then made twenty-two kayaks in only two weeks. They were so devoted to their projects that they started before 7 A.M. and worked past 10 P.M. except for attending classes they couldn't miss. At night I often had to take tools away from students in order get them to quit. Our kayaking and camping adventure along the California Desert wilderness was a great first for all of us. Our high school principal said it was the most highly motivated class he had ever seen in his long career.

Woodshop Electricians

A group of woodworking students became interested adding needed electrical wall outlets and 12' ceiling drops to our shop. With a local electrician as adviser, they worked in class, before and after school and during lunch. The cadre of four "electricians" could not be kept away from their project. Next they did the welding shop. In a professional manner, outlets were installed "everywhere". There was safety in our shops and lifetime skills for these "Electricians."

Learning Virtues

Hug- A-Board

After my woodworking students cut a board for their first project we conducted our "Hug A Board" ceremony. In a spirit of **reverence** and **gratitude** students hugged their boards while I delivered a two minute "sermon" describing the tree's miraculous creation and the efforts of many workers in protecting, harvesting, transporting, milling, drying and marketing their precious piece of wood. "Hug your board, and let the fun begin in making a high quality heirloom project for your future grandchildren."

Thank You

Early in my second teaching career, it became apparent that students lacked feelings and expressions of **gratitude**. I began a practice, after helping a student, of kindly saying, "Thank you very much, Mr. Ross, for helping me with my project." Before long the students caught on and started sincerely expressing their gratitude for help they received.

Chapter 6
What to Learn?

Experiencing the wealth of abilities within each student is the most beneficial goal of learning in our schools. As personal attributes are realized the desire and need to acquire more diversity and depth in learning emerges. Development of the unique traits of each student results in the greatest personal and societal benefit. It is the key to achieving self worth, creativity and positive behavior. Nurturing personal qualities is much more important than acquiring academic information.

The answer for enhancing the desire to learn is matching useful activities with the innate abilities of the individual student. This is very challenging, if not impossible, in light of traditional and habitual school practices. It is a necessary goal if we are to experience the wealth within each student. The following concepts are offered for consideration in developing programs that nurture individual attributes so students can experience the best of themselves and life.

Interwoven in all learning activities should be the fundamentals of The Pattern of Human Behavior that result in positive behavior. Readily receiving and sharing is practiced by helping each other which also provides the best way to enjoy personal attributes. Useful activities provide the best goal for accomplishing these qualities. The following concepts are offered for consideration in developing effective learning programs.

Helping Each Other

We are social beings who gather in groups to help each other in teamwork fashion. The skills involved in helping each other are essential to successful activities. It is learned in activities with others and is the best way to promote learning of common interest. Students enjoy and share their attributes in a most productive way when helping each other. The skill is vital for our survival and prosperity.

Amish communities of the Midwestern States exemplify this practice. Within their families, schools, churches and communities, helping each other is basic to their way of life. Plowing, planting, harvesting, building, quilting, cleaning, food preserving and cooking are done in family and friendship groups. They seldom operate alone which results in a very wholesome way of life.

Enjoying Personal Attributes

It is of greatest value for students to learn the enjoyment of personal attributes. They are the soul of our being. Enjoying and sharing personal attributes is likely the ultimate life experience.

Project Completion

Life is a series of projects; some small, some large, some easy and some challenging. Projects are individual or group ventures to achieve a particular goal. Large projects involve working with many people and may last several years. Students may start alone with small projects and progress to larger projects in groups. Further development involves several groups working together.

Curriculum

Useful curriculum is based on real life needs. Over many years of careful observation, I have identified six Basic Life Activities for consideration in curriculum development: 1) Good Self Health, 2) Employment Careers, 3) Communication, 4) Social Relationships, 5) Environmental Harmony and 6) Aesthetic Enjoyments.

Basic Life Activities

Good Self Health

Good health is the most significant factor for personal well-being. Without good health, everything else in life is diminished. Our health is primarily a personal responsibility. We determine our movement or exercise and what we put into our lungs and mouth. Rest, hygiene and medical responses are determined by each individual. It is obvious that we have not learned to practice the fundamentals of good self health as indicated by our soaring health problems.

*Our own bodies are the most important
thing for which we can care.*

In attaining good health exercise is very important. Without movement we die. Exercise increases our consumption of the air and its essential oxygen. It is the first element needed for us to live. Normally, we cannot live for more than a few minutes without oxygen. From the air we breath, it is free. Consider: the more oxygen we consume, the healthier we will be. Exercise increases the flow of our nutritious blood to the extremities of our circulatory system. It also brings balance to the rest of our health needs. Poor habits of exercise and consumption are huge problems among many youth and adults.

Schools have neglected the learning of good health habits. Little credence is given to exercise. Few students experience the pleasures of fine physical condition. As our society has become more sedentary, our schools have reduced time for exercise instead of increasing it.

Students need to develop good consumption habits in the use of air, water and food. It is important for them to understand the harms of alcohol, tobacco and drugs. Instead of dealing with the root problem in developing good self health habits, expensive medicines and medical procedures proliferate, sometimes to the detriment of our health.

*Every student should learn to practice
qualities of healthy living every day.*

Employment Careers

Good employment is essential for personal fulfillment and the general welfare. Work is natural for all creatures in their quest for food and shelter. Pleasures beyond food and shelter are realized through work.

The highest of seven Jewish charity levels is to help others learn a vocation. As the Chinese proverb says; "Give a man a fish and you feed him for a day. Teach him to fish and you feed him for a lifetime."

It is tragic that so little attention is given to the identification and development of employment skills. Few students leave school having made a career choice or developed employment skills. They go through life working at jobs for which they are unsuited. According to statistics, 8 out of 10 people dislike their jobs. Employers struggle to find employees with the needed skills. This need not be the case.

Many years ago, I became interested in identifying the basic employment career fields. Through much study, these four basic career fields resulted: 1) Creating Careers, 2) Manufacturing Careers, 3) Servicing Careers, and 4) Marketing Careers. Basic skills and career clusters are defined for each field. When shown the results, business people said, "This is exactly what we do."

Creating Careers

Creating careers involve the planning or designing of procedures, products and services. Employment opportunities are quite limited in creating careers. Considerable experience is needed and designs are often used for long periods. The six basic skills of creating careers are: 1) Identifying Problems, 2) Formulating Ideas, 3) Gathering Resources, 4) Recording Ideas, 5) Refining Ideas and 6) Presenting the product.

Creating career clusters include: 1) Communications, 2) Structures, 3) Substances and 4) Productions.

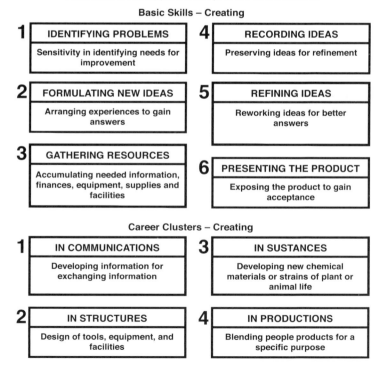

The Creating Careers

Planning or designing procedures, products and/or services

Basic Skills – Creating

1 IDENTIFYING PROBLEMS
Sensitivity in identifying needs for improvement

4 RECORDING IDEAS
Preserving ideas for refinement

2 FORMULATING NEW IDEAS
Arranging experiences to gain answers

5 REFINING IDEAS
Reworking ideas for better answers

3 GATHERING RESOURCES
Accumulating needed information, finances, equipment, supplies and facilities

6 PRESENTING THE PRODUCT
Exposing the product to gain acceptance

Career Clusters – Creating

1 IN COMMUNICATIONS
Developing information for exchanging information

3 IN SUSTANCES
Developing new chemical materials or strains of plant or animal life

2 IN STRUCTURES
Design of tools, equipment, and facilities

4 IN PRODUCTIONS
Blending people products for a specific purpose

Manufacturing Careers

Manufacturing careers involve processing materials to create useful products. This is the second largest employment area. Virtually all food, clothing, pharmaceuticals, tools, machines, vehicles, toys, furniture, equipment and buildings are manufactured. Individuals, who like to make things, enjoy manufacturing. These are the five basic skills of manufacturing: 1) Material Handling, 2) Quality Control, 3) Conditioning Materials, 4) Fabricating Parts, 5) Assembling Parts and 6) Finishing.

Career clusters include: 1) Mass Production and 2) Craft Production.

The Manufacturing Careers

Processing materials to produce useful products

Basic Skills – Manufacturing

1 | MATERIAL HANDLING
Contain and move masses

4 | FABRICATING PARTS
Cutting and forming materials

2 | QUALITY CONTROL
Evaluating items to specifications

5 | ASSEMBLING PARTS
Connecting pieces

3 | CONDITIONING MATERIALS
Modifying the state of materials

6 | FINISHING
Applying a coating to surfaces

Career Clusters – Manufacturing

1 | MASS PRODUCTION
A team of people making quantities of a product

2 | CRAFT PRODUCTION
A single person making a single product

Servicing Careers

Servicing careers entail the care of people, products and data. They represent the largest and fastest growing field of employment. There are five basic skills of servicing careers: 1) Establishing Rapport, 2) Planning the Service Procedure, 3) Procurement of Service Components, 4) Conducting the Service and 5) Evaluating the Results.

Servicing career clusters include: 1) People, 2) Products and 3) Data.

The Servicing Careers

Care of people, products and/or data

Basic Skills – Servicing

1 ESTABLISHING RAPPORT	**4** CONDUCTING
Developing relationships of common purpose with participants	Activating the participants to accomplish the purpose of the program

2 PLANNING	**5** EVALUATING
Developing a scheme for accomplishing the purpose of a program	Assessing the results of the program in terms of the purpose

3 PROCURING
Obtaining and readying components for the program

Career Clusters – Servicing

1 WITH PEOPLE	**3** WITH DATA
Providing expertise to associates in fields of education, sales, medical, grooming, recreation, entertainment, textiles or plants	Processing words, numbers, symbols, lines, shades and textures, record and provide information

2 WITH PRODUCTS
Maintaining and repairing facilities, mechanical or electrical equipment, textiles or plants

Marketing Careers

Marketing activities involve acquiring, pricing, controlling, selling and distributing designs, products and services. Often marketing personnel never come in contact with the products or services involved. Their work involves use of data communicated to suppliers and customers. Marketing employment is quite small and selective. Communication and record keeping skills are of great importance. The seven basic skills of marketing are: 1) Searching Information, 2) Developing Information, 3) Controlling Information, 4) Financing, 5) Purchasing, 6) Pricing, 7) Selling and 8) Distributing.

Marketing career clusters include; 1) Brokerage, 2) Wholesale, 3) Retail, 4) Mail Order, 5) Internet, 6) Phone, 7) Import and 8) Export.

The Marketing Careers

Acquiring, controlling, selling and distributing designs, products and services

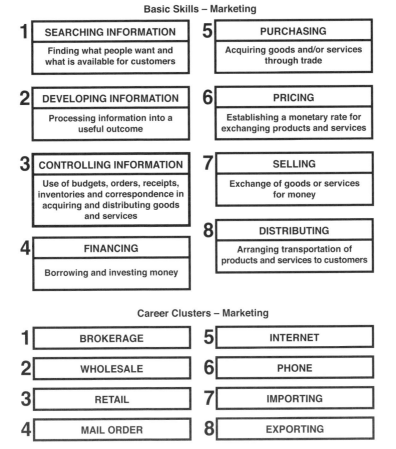

Basic Skills – Marketing

1 SEARCHING INFORMATION
Finding what people want and what is available for customers

2 DEVELOPING INFORMATION
Processing information into a useful outcome

3 CONTROLLING INFORMATION
Use of budgets, orders, receipts, inventories and correspondence in acquiring and distributing goods and services

4 FINANCING
Borrowing and investing money

5 PURCHASING
Acquiring goods and/or services through trade

6 PRICING
Establishing a monetary rate for exchanging products and services

7 SELLING
Exchange of goods or services for money

8 DISTRIBUTING
Arranging transportation of products and services to customers

Career Clusters – Marketing

1 BROKERAGE
2 WHOLESALE
3 RETAIL
4 MAIL ORDER
5 INTERNET
6 PHONE
7 IMPORTING
8 EXPORTING

Career Ladders

There is an ever more demanding sequence of jobs within each employment field known as a career ladder. At the bottom are the least demanding skills. As progress is made up each rung, skills become more demanding. The skills at the bottom are known as entry-level. These should be learned first. When entry-level skills are attained, employment may be sought. Early employment is important as one can learn a great deal by being in the work environment. Combining work experience with school is far more valuable than school alone. Too often entry-level jobs are considered poor. This is not true. The basic experiences are highly beneficial to future achievement. Work provides contact with the employee network which is helpful for future jobs and learning. Virtually all entry-level jobs can lead to top level employment.

Career ladders may start in a store, factory, farm, hospital, construction sites, etc. Beginning as a cleaning person can be a great start in progressing on a career ladder. The experience helps in relating to other workers and knowing the business from the ground up. Such basic involvement also provides the practical, hands-on experience that is fundamental to creative endeavors.

Employment Realities

It is stressed in schools that more education results in more income. Missing in this premise is the fact that the average ability varies significantly from group to group. Employment success often depends more on inherent ability than upon the amount of schooling. The facts are:

1) Some high school dropouts earn more money than high school or college graduates.
2) Some high school graduates earn more money than college graduates.
3) Some college dropouts earn more money than college graduates.
4) Some college undergraduates earn more money than higher degree graduates.

One does not need to go to college to be successful. Academic education is over sold while practical experience is under stressed. There always have been, and there always will be, highly successful people who have not attended college. For many careers college education is of little value. It is costly in time and money. Unless a career choice requires a college degree for licensing, one should not fret over lack of a college degree.

There are many good ways to learn life skills other than in schools.

One-half of the engineers producing the Apollo Spacecraft were not college graduates. They were experienced and talented machinists, mechanics and drafters who rose to engineering positions. Retail clerks can become store managers. Inventors and entrepreneurial individuals develop highly successful businesses without college degrees.

Communication

Communication is always among the top problems in human activity. Yet, it is not a school subject. There are subjects related to communication but little reflecting everyday practices. The closest school curriculum comes to dealing with communication is English and mathematics classes. English classes follow an academic curriculum and do not address practical communication needs. Mathematics classes lack practical application of fundamentals. This failure is evident in the fact that many graduates are unable to use mathematics accurately in employment and daily use.

Through communication, information is exchanged. It is accomplished by voice, sounds, printed words, numbers, symbols, drawings, models, music, motions and pictures. In life, communication is often a group effort involving writers, artists, editors, proof-readers, photographers, model makers, printers, speakers, actors and producers; a teaming of talents. A single concept may require pictures, technical drawings, maps, charts, graphs, formulas, models and even cartoons to best communicate.

In manufacturing businesses, models of automobiles, aircraft, appliances and buildings are used as the ultimate communication media. Models exhibit accurate life-like vision and operation of products. They provide much more than words or diagrams can depict. With technical writing, illustrations are vital to producing literature used in production, assembly, operation and maintenance of products. Life activities require reading and making technical drawings, maps, charts and graphs; yet these are not included in the common curriculum.

In school, all mathematics problems come from books. In life few mathematics problems come from books. Mathematics is the science of measurement but there are no measuring tools, instruments or data gathering activities included in classes. As a result, graduates have great difficult with the practical application of mathematics.

Status is almost exclusively given to words and numbers while other learning is held in lower esteem. Other abilities go unaddressed. Actually a broad range of communication skills are needed in life.

Through our wonderful ability to communicate we develop social relationships.

Social Relationships

Social relationships involve individuals associating with each other. Good results happen through effective communication and virtuous behavior. Helping each other is fundamental to successful social relationships. It is not an integral part of classes. Important social skills involve marriage relationships and child nurturing. Within twelve years of required social studies there is no significant effort given to these basic needs.

It is obvious that we are not getting along with each other as we are capable. The cost to our nation is staggering and globally unsustainable.

The skills of planning and conducting programs are not learned in the present dictated curriculum. The fundamentals for doing this are next covered in Chapter 7; Linking Students, Learning and Life.

Environmental Harmony

Our environment involves everything around us. It is all encompassing with each component related, interdependent, different and changing. Our well-being depends upon understanding and caring for the environment. Students need practical experiences involving the environment to better their lives and understand the consequences of their activities. In life science classes students have very little experience in caring for plants and creatures. How can students really learn about life and not care directly for plants and creatures? To be effective, the fundamentals of science need to be learned through practical experiences.

Aesthetic Enjoyments

Aesthetic enjoyments involve the use or observation of talents in a recreational and leisurely fashion. They include; music, art, games, dances, sports, drama, literature, travel and wandering. Participation and spectatorship in a variety of aesthetic enjoyments brings balance to one's life. Often they provide change-of-pace in activity which fosters enlightenment for creative solutions. For many participants, aesthetic enjoyments provide the best outlet for creativity. Employment opportunities are quite limited but for a few they can be very rewarding.

Students benefit greatly by having aesthetics as an integral part of every school day. This is especially true of music, which is fundamental to human development and enjoyment. The playing of selected classical music has been found to be very beneficial to the intellectual development of infants, toddlers, students and adults. Some years ago, the state of Georgia started a practice of issuing a classical CD to the parents of each newborn child. The different themes of the music nurture specific aspects of a child's activities.

Music can well be considered a universal language. Its qualities have worldwide understanding and enjoyment. Music can be composed, read and interpreted with common meaning throughout humankind. Participation in music group performances, such as, orchestra, chorus and band, is one of the very best learning experiences for students. Music is to be an important part of every school day.

Every student is capable of becoming proficient to their personal level of enjoyment in several aesthetic activities. It is during times of aesthetic enjoyment that creative solutions are often hatched. They are wonderful change of pace activities.

Summary

Helping each other and nurturing of student attributes can be integrated into most learning activities. Basic life activities provide the source for useful learning.

Learnings Along the Way

Practical Science

In developing career programs, I became interested in entry-level employment opportunities in science laboratories: jobs that did not require a college degree. There were four major scientific research centers in our service area. We hired a science teacher from one of our 19 high schools to explore the field and develop a curriculum. He had considerable practical science experience and spent much of the summer interviewing personnel in science laboratories determining skill and employment needs. Upon completing the research and curriculum we discussed the proposed class with one of our high school principals, a former science teacher. After reviewing the work, the principal asked, "Where in the curriculum would our experienced science students begin studies." The science teacher said, "At the beginning. There is nothing in this class that students learn in our science classes."

Teaching English - Communication

At one point in my career I wanted to teach English which in reality would be a Communications class. My plan was to clear the classroom of everything. Upon arriving the students would be faced with an apparent need. What do we want to do? What do we want to learn? What furniture, equipment, supplies and literature do we need? How are we going to solve our needs? Students could bring folding chairs and tables from home on a borrowed basis until we could make better arrangements. Can you imagine the attention these students would get at home, in the community and at school as they brought the folding chairs and tables to school? They would be off and running with wonderful learning adventures. Organization, planning, projects, fundraising, literature, a phone and a wealth of communication development would be in order.

In sharing this idea, people always want to know how it worked out. Unfortunately, I never had the opportunity to carry out the plan as other career opportunities developed.

Chapter 8
From Teacher to Facilitator of Learning

I think of my early years when I taught beginning drafting and the use of basic tools employed in making simple drawings. By the end of the year the students were quite skilled. The next year in the drafting II class, this skilled student resource was isolated from beginners. Skilled students could not use their abilities to help others learn. With years of university, industrial and teaching experience I was, by myself, again teaching the most elemental aspects of drafting to beginning students. What a waste of learning opportunities for the experienced students. They could have better helped beginners and greatly increased their own abilities in the process. Think of the self-worth and skills they would have gained in helping the beginners.

Eighteen years later, after 15 years of administration and three years in private business, I conducted my classes much differently. The great student resource was utilized for learning as they freely helped each other.

Changing from the traditional teacher to facilitator of learning makes the work much more enjoyable, productive and rewarding for teachers and students. It requires a change in attitude and an understanding of the differences in the roles. The adjustment is fundamentally from "command and control" or "herding" to facilitator of learning. The new role entails the creation of an environment that maximizes learning. Instead of it emanating primarily from the teacher and textbooks, the entire class becomes involved in the teaching/learning process. As a result, accomplishment increases while problems of motivation, discipline and attendance are nearly eliminated.

The role is similar to that of the one room school teacher where students learn a great deal from each other. Making use of the natural diversity stimulates wholesome learning. This is very different from the attempted homogeneous grouping, row seating and chapter-by-chapter of traditional practices. In the customary role it is humanly impossible for the teacher to serve the diverse needs of each student.

*Results are amazing when students are
involved in helping each other learn.*

The following fundamentals are defined for consideration in fulfilling the facilitator of learning role:

Student Qualities
  1) Each student is different from all others.
  2) Each student has an abundance of unique inborn attributes.
  3) Each student has a natural desire, ability and need to learn.
  4) Each student has a primary need for identity be it positive or negative.
  5) Students benefit most by first learning through practical experiences.
  6) Students have a desire and need to socialize by sharing.

Student Needs
  1) Good Self Health Habits
  2) Employment Career Skills
  3) Communication Skills
  4) Social Relationship Skills
  5) Environmental Harmony Practices
  6) Aesthetic Enjoyments

These qualities and needs are addressed through The Multi-Purpose Program component of The Management for Learning Concept. Facilitators (teachers) of learning may need help in planning and conducting the programs. This may require in-service and will involve:

  1) Developing *Learning Activity Schedules* using flow charts and/or graphic networks to provide a variety of learning opportunities.

  2) Formulating *Personnel Organization Plans* composed of students having similar interests with varying experience levels.

3) *Arranging the Environment* in learning centers equipped, furnished and supplied to provide for the desired activities of the students.

With commitment to transformation of our schools we can orchestrate a harmonious learning experience for all students.

Learnings Along the Way

Erik's Timing with Teaching

Erik is a high school junior who helps me with use of my computer. He has an uncanny ability in helping me learn. When I have difficulty performing a task, he waits until I have considered two or three options. At the appropriate time, before frustration sets in, Erik says, "You might try this _____," or he shows me the way. Frustration or feelings of failure are avoided. When after considering several options, I perform correctly, he gives me a shy smile or joins me in the laughter of success. It seems he gets as much joy from this as me.

I mentioned this remarkable quality to his mother as a compliment about her son. She said, "Erik learned that while helping his younger brother learn the more advanced mathematics that Erik was learning in school."

Learning Later

My first year of teaching, I tried repeatedly to help the few seventh grade students who could not accurately measure with a 1/16" marked ruler. They were not able to learn the skill. Eventually, I gave up. In a mysterious way they were able to do their projects to satisfaction. As eighth graders the same students learned the skill with ease.

From this I learned to give students a fair try at learning and then go on. They will learn it later if able. Why rub their nose in the problem?

Staying Out of Learning's Way

Kevin, an exceptionally talented student, had turned a beautiful walnut bowl on the lathe. He asked me if he could turn a lid for it. I inquired what he had in mind. He drew a sketch showing pie-shaped segments glued together in a way that I had not seen. My first thought questioned whether it would work. Fortunately my second thought was, with his ability it may work. So I said, "Try it." His idea worked very well. As a result of not getting in the way of Kevin's learning, my students and I enjoyed making turnings using the same technique for years.

Moving Lumber

When wood shop students carried lumber from the delivery truck to the lumber room, I noticed that their "loads" varied considerably. Two students carried one board while another carried four boards. I talked to the "slackers" about the differences in earnings, if they were employed as piece workers. As a result, lumber began moving much faster. I saw vividly that some students really hadn't learned to work.

Gold or Silver Star?

I conducted wood shop with beginning, intermediate and advanced students mixed in the same class. A practice of awarding gold or silver starts was conducted, especially with my "ragmuffin" students. When they did an especially good job, I praised them and asked if they would like a gold or silver star. In their first such experience rookies always chose the gold star, which I awarded in the form of a penny. After that opportunity they always wanted a silver star; nickel, dime or quarter. Occasionally, after helping a student, they would say, "Mr. Ross, you did a good job. Do you want a gold or silver star?" "Silver." A dime to my hand.

From Scowl to Star

Margaret entered my wood shop class mid-semester facing me with a very hostile look. My thought was, "I will transform that scowl into a smile of confidence here." Within weeks, Margaret was engaging in class, and the rest of school, becoming a good and likeable student. Two years later, while she was turning a wooden bowl on a lathe, I visited with her. It was near the end of the period, just before Christmas. I discussed how well she had done over the past two years and she smilingly agreed. Then I asked Margaret if she wanted a gold or silver star. She quickly said, "Silver." I handed her a silver dollar, my first such pricey award. She was so excited and appreciative. Within minutes after the class, you can be sure, many of the students and staff knew about Margaret's prize. I wonder where she is now? She hasn't forgotten, I'm sure.

Chapter 9
Improving Our Schools

First and foremost, the government and universities must change their roles in regard to their involvement with our schools. Their stranglehold on our students' learning opportunities must be eliminated. Significant change cannot take place unless this happens. With their dictates removed, effective learning may become a reality. Student experiences can become practical and creative.

Curriculum has evolved with little or no regard to genuine needs. It is greatly generated by commercial textbook and test publishers. The result is a deplorable waste of human effort and money as publishers and universities prosper while students, teachers and society lose.

Schools have no thorough follow-up studies with alumni to assess the value of their schooling. The type of research needed to determine these needs would certainly be wonderful learning experiences for social studies and business students. It is done routinely in business activities and would be a beneficial skill when seeking employment. Students could be involved with mail, telephone and personal surveys. A survey of alumni might cover the following:

1) What did you learn that was particularly useful?
2) What learning was not used?
3) What were their unmet needs?

The actual job needs can be researched with employers in a like manner. This information is also available from the United States Department of Labor, Dictionary of Occupational Titles which describes reading, mathematics and other job requirements.

Data gathered could be deciphered and presented by students and used in revising learning activities. Such activities provide a real world experience.

Other considerations for improving our schools may include:

1. Change schools from educational or teaching institutions to learning programs. This would help break away from the traditions and mind-sets that inhibit improvement.

2. Identify both students and teachers with natural leadership qualities and involve them in leadership training programs.

3. Identify students and teachers who are especially helpful with others and conduct workshops to improve their skills as well as share their skills with others.

4. Develop a peer support program having students of various interests, abilities and grade levels in groups of six or eight in each homeroom. Home rooms would have four to six groups. Each group would have a facilitator. Activity would start with sharing problems and successes followed by problem solving. Students having difficulty in one group would change to another group. Service projects in the school or community could be done. Facilitators would be organized to share their group experiences with others.

5. Bridge English, mathematics, science, and social studies curriculum from academic to practical learning experiences.

6. Change the mind-set role of traditional teaching to facilitator of learning. A program is needed to free educators from the present restrictive and ineffective practices.

7. Utilize the student resource for learning.

8. Reduce subject requirements so students could respond to their personal qualities and needs with electives.

9. Involve students in the total school operation as learning activities. This may include:

   a. Custodial Services
   b. Food Services
   c. Learning Aides
   d. Counseling Aides
   e. Office Clerks
   f. Landscaping
   g. Maintenance
   h. Construction

   i. Cashiering
   j. Administration
   k. Medical Services
   l. Curriculum Development
   m. Publicity
   n. Welfare
   o. Safety and Security
   p. Research

10. Consider using the entire community for learning instead of just the school properties.

11. Use citizens of the community as a learning resource.

12. Recognize the achievements of all students, not just the academic achievers. No losers!

Involving students, staff and citizens in identifying, planning and implementing school improvements can certainly produce better results than we are now experiencing.

> *After several evaluations one of my clever students handed me his project and said, "Mr. Ross, I don't want to make it any better so I have room for improvement."*

This work is offered with room for improvement. It is my hope that together we can make our schools better for students and society. There is plenty of room for improvement.

Learnings Along the Way

Never Too Late for First Book

Pete was a successful restaurant owner, wonderful family man and very charitable citizen. During Pete's rehabilitation from knee replacement I shared a favorite book with him entitled *Life Is So Good* by George Dawson and Richard Glaubman. "One man's extra ordinary journey through the 20th century and how he learned to read at 98." Upon returning it, Pete said that it was the first book he ever read cover to cover. When I asked him to sign the book with this fact, he at first refused, replying, "I don't want people to know how dumb I am." Being good friends I jokingly said, "Pete everyone in town knows." He signed the book. "This is a good book. It's the first book I ever read, cover to cover, in my life. I'm now 78 years old! Pete."

Tears of joy come as I write this and I am
not even a reading teacher.

From Problem Reader to Engineer

A fifth grade teacher told Jim's Mother to take him to the library every week to choose a book to read in an effort to improve his poor reading skill. Jim picked out the thinnest book with the biggest print he could find. Jim remembers it 68 years later as a book about a unicorn. He liked animals, especially dogs. Next trip he found a thin, large print book about dogs which lead him to reading every dog book in the library. Next came, horses, African animals and a lifetime of avid reading including classics. Without college, Jim became an engineer, trouble-shooting mechanical power transmission equipment problems throughout the United States and Canada for the Dodge Manufacturing Company, Mishawaka, Indiana, maker of industrial power transmission equipment.

The Board Stretcher Ceremonial

My brother, Milt, was revered by his students with many stories about funny happenings. He was a stickler for accurate measurements to prevent wasted materials.

With fellow shop teachers, he rigged up a "board stretching" contraption which was kept in the print shop storage room. In one particular incident, when a board was cut short, the student was sent to retrieve the "board stretcher." After placing the contraption on the work bench with the board installed, Milt got a bright idea. Remembering a large piece of purple satin cloth that had found its way to the shop rag container, he fetched the satin and covered the board stretcher for a ceremonial. All 22 students were gathered around the bench and told to close their eyes, slowly raise and lower their arms in front of them and hum. With great respect and admiration for my brother, the "swaggers," "rag-a-muffins," and "sharpies" all went along with the ritual. That is, until Milt burst out laughing joined by his beloved students. Imagine the sight and the remembrances of this off-the-wall experience.

The Dowel

In wood shop a student asked Milt for a 3/8" diameter, six-inch long birch dowel. The student said they had looked in the box of short dowels but there were none there. They both looked to no avail. In the lumber room they found a new 3/8" x 36" long dowel. The student went to his work bench to cut the 6" piece. A few minutes later the student returned saying he couldn't get the dowel into the workbench vise. Milt went to the student's bench to find the vise extended out to its full 15" capacity instead of the 3/8" capacity necessary for securing the piece for cutting.

The Too-Sharp Plane

A student in my brother's woodshop came to him and said, "My wood plane is too sharp." Milt was pretty curious about a plane being too-sharp, especially in the school shop. He went to the student's workbench where the board had been worked by the too-sharp plane. The observation revealed that the edge of the board was chipped due to planing in the wrong direction, against the grain. So much for the too-sharp plane.

Extreme Care

Joe's beautiful jewelry box never touched the work bench, vise jaws or storage locker during its entire construction process. He brought a nice tan Turkish towel to class and from the beginning, the boards and the box never left the protective wrap of his towel. Great respect for the value of boards and projects was learned from Joe's unusual care of his work.

Superintendent's Questioning

After review of a course outline for a proposed Construction class, my superintendent questioned why moving materials was included as one of the first skills to be learned. The inference was that anyone could move building materials. Why take school time to learn that? As simple as it may seem, moving materials involves special skills that are important to construction costs. Beginning laborers usually do such work and those who move the materials efficiently are likely to move up the career ladder. It's the "simple" basics that are important to entry-level employment and beyond.

T. J., Our Research Analyst

With our fast growing Regional Occupational Program we had need for a Research Analyst. Conversion of attendance and financial data into charts and graphs was required to better manage the operation. We also wanted someone who could do library research. Customarily this position would be filled by a college graduate.

We developed a job description based upon that of the United States Department of Labor's Dictionary of Occupational Titles. The announcement was distributed to students by our high school counselors. Nearly 20 students applied and five were interviewed for the minimum wage position. Two of the candidates related, "My parents said I should take this position even if it didn't pay anything."

We selected T. J., who performed ideally. His work primarily involved adding, subtracting, multiplying and dividing along with incorporating the results on charts and graphs. After several weeks of the rather routine work, I said to T. J., "I am sorry we don't have more challenging things for you to do." He responded, "That's okay, I see how useful my work is toward the program's success."

Later, we shared the data materials with other administrators who asked how we had time to develop such useful conclusions. I said, "We have a Research Analyst." Their reply was, "You guys have everything. How do you afford it?" I responded, "He is a part-time high school student."

T. J. continued this work through his junior and senior years, then changed his college plans to stay with the program while attending a local university.

Shoveling 101

As I drove across our school district parking lot, I observed three construction class students beside a 4' x 6' hole in the pavement. One was barely digging while the others watched and held up their shovels. I wanted to talk and demonstrate the "joys" of shoveling to them but decided better of it and left that to their teacher. My brother and I used to race the clock and each other digging numerous 4' x 6' x 6' holes for heating oil tanks in construction. We had grown up digging holes for shacks and forts in vacant lots. These students were not lazy; they just had no experience digging holes. Each following day the students' participation improved. At the next school board meeting, I related the situation. Jokingly, I suggested that we start a Shoveling 101 class. We had a good laugh, although the problem is serious, for shoveling is a basic skill for construction.

Drill Cord

Late in my career I was wrapping the cord around the body of an electric drill. As usual, the cord was not staying in place. A student said, "Here Mr. Ross, I'll show you how to do that." He wrapped the cord in a figure 8 around the body and handle of the drill. I nearly always think of that student's teaching whenever wrapping tool cords.

Forced Learning – No Way

Brandon was a light hearted very likeable seventh-grade student who was two years behind his grade level. After a couple of lessons dealing with using a ruler in drafting class, Brandon could not read the measurements. I felt it important that he learn the skill so I gave him special attention. After a couple of tries he still could not read the ruler, so Brandon became my special project. I plotted different approaches every day or so. After other tries Brandon would say, "Mr. Ross, you know I don't want to learn that." Another plot, another, "Mr. Ross, you know I don't want to learn that." I learned a valuable teaching lesson from Brandon.

"Forcing" students to learn what they are incapable of doing or don't want to learn is wasted effort. Help them find wholesome things they want to learn.

Table Saw Adventures

Within 20 minutes of entering our wood shop at the beginning of each semester, students were gathered around the best of our three table saws observing the procedures for safely cutting boards. For some it was review. For others it was the beginning experience. Within a few more minutes the students were lined up waiting their turn to learn. I didn't see much value in having students spend a lot of class time with lecturing, reading, writing and written tests in a shop full of tools, machines, and lumber as well as project possibilities. Students wanted to make projects without a bunch of side issues. Watching other students practice helped them learn the process. As activity progressed, I selected a skilled advanced student to help learners at the first saw. I then took a group of the waiting students to the next saw for the same procedure. This was repeated again to the third table saw. My focus was always on the entire operation. With all three groups being lead by advanced students, it was a pleasure to watch the abundant learning taking place. Can you imagine the excitement at the evening dinner table when the students were asked what they did in their first day back to school? "I learned to cut boards safely on a table saw in shop class."

Trailers to Terrariums — Special Education

As our Regional Occupational Program grew we saw the need to help Special Education students learn job skills. We hired a teacher during the summer to outfit a large trailer with different learning areas that represented a cross section of the world of work. The teacher, with woodworking students, constructed cabinetry and installed the equipment. Utility hook-ups were placed at Special Education sites. The program proved so successful that we soon prepared a second trailer and hired a teacher. With their individual creativity, differing programs developed. One project of particular merit was the mass production and sale of terrariums. A variety of plants were purchased in large quantities, along with soil and attractive glass containers. Terrariums were mass produced, with each student doing one of several tasks. The supervisor of the program made an appointment for one of the students to come to my office. The young girl arrived with the supervisor. In a halting, deeply caring manner, she said, "Mr...President (I was Superintendent), we...want to...thank you very much...for our beau...tiful...trailer... We have made...this very...nice terrarium...for you." I thanked her and asked if I could go see their trailer. She asked the supervisor, who said, "Yes." As their car stopped at the trailer, she popped out and virtually skidded around the corners getting the back door of the trailer to meet me at the front door. What a bunch of very happy kids there were, with dozens of beautiful terrariums. An indelible experience for all of us.

Our Company

LIFE LEARNING LLC

We promote life learning activities and publications in teamwork relationships that enhance participant abilities. This is accomplished through speaking engagements, motivational lectures, training workshops, consultations and coaching.

Our illustrated speaking topics include:

1) Transforming Schools to Serve Student and Community Needs
2) Schools in Crisis?
3) Establishing Positive Behavior
4) How We Learn
5) What to Learn
6) Management for Learning
7) From Teacher to Facilitator of Learning

Assistance is given to authors in developing and publishing materials that nurture the unique attributes of individuals. All of our efforts are "down to earth" and free of academic jargon.

Business activities are conducted as much as practical by high school and college students with experienced adults in support. Profits are used for charitable activities involving life learning endeavors. Our efforts are neutral relative to religion and politics.

In progress is a personal development book entitled CREATING JOY along with publications detailing concepts presented in TRANSFORMING OUR SCHOOLS.

We are very much interested in the life learning incidents and activities of others. Your suggestions, comments, stories and works are solicited. Through sharing we can be most helpful in bettering ourselves and others.

Thank you very much for your interest in our activities and publications.

Life Learning LLC
138 River Avenue
Mishawaka, IN 46544

Phone: (574) 255-2425
Email: LifeLearning@live.com